SACHIN TENDULKAR COLOUR

INDIAN CRICKETER

MR VIVEK KUMAR PANDEY SHAMBHUNATH

Short biography of Sachin Tendulkar and about life.During writing this book no character & no religious are harmed written by Mr Vivek Kumar Pandey. winner youngest writer award 1st rank in india 2020.He is only one writer can publish 700+ own book that was greatest successfull in his life .This book fully colour edition books.

Contents

Foreword

Author biography in English :MY NAME IS VIVEK KUMAR PANDEY . I WAS BORN IN 30 SEP 2002,I AM FROM SURAT GUJARAT INDIA.MY DREAM WAS TO BE GOOD WRITERS ,MY FAMILY SUPPORTED ME TO SUCCESSFUL AND I CAN DO IT MY SELF.How do I write? That is a question, I believe, that cannot be honestly answered by me."CELEBRATING YOUNGEST WRITER AWARD WINNER IN GUJARAT 1ST RANK" MR PANDEY JI . I may think I did a good job writing something when in reality it could be horrible. The reader is the one who decides the quality of my writing. I do not find writing to be natural to me and therefore find it to be a real challenge. My trick as a challenged writer is to do the best I can and know that I am happy with the final outcome. It may take a while to do my best and there may be quite a few problems I run into along the way.

I am not a greedy person those who are thinking about me and my self I never tried it anyone people suffering from sadness ,I trying to get promoted people suffering from happiness and joy in your Life Time. Now in current situation in India and also world people are unemployed and have no many but our indian governor help to people to get free food from ration card , i also take part in leadership team ,i am Motivational speaker , Film script writer. There was my two dream firstly writer and secondly actor & also my own film is upcoming soon i done almost completely completed script for my film .I AM GOING TO SAY WORD OF HEART TOUCH OUT PLEASE READ IT" , firstly i thanks my father he supports me in this field they always getting inspired me by own his words and behavior ,they always said that he was a biggest person in the world in future and also they purchase fruit and chocolate for me in anytime & anyway , firstly my father buy him then call me Vivek you want a chocolate i will say yes papa but how many tell me ,papa: you tell me how much i buy him i told 1 or 2 chocolate but my father purchase whole the boxes of chocolate and they get suprised me. MY FATHER WAS BORN IN " 20 SEPTEMBER" 1971 IN INDIA.

1) MY FATHER FAVORITE CLOTHES IS KURTA PAIJMA AND ALSO STYLES SHOE

2) FAVORITE SINGER IS KISHORE DA

3) FAVORITE STATE GUJARAT AND KOLKATA , HIS VILLAGE IN BIHAR

4) FAVORITE COLOR BLACK AND WHITE

THEY ALSO LOVE cricket like IPL and one day t-20 .they also like watching a News daily and heard the song daily ,they also interested in tik tok video but in current time tik tok is banned in india but also few videos are in you tube. In lockdown time my family and me very enjoy day daily. my father play daily ludo with his sister and son, daughter.they always loved tea and coffee anytime call me "। वविंक थोडा़ चाय बनाओना वविंक तुम्हारे हाथ का चाय अच्छा लगता है". I make it tea for my father but some reason after the April to june they are suffering from fever and cough , weakness on 6 June 2020 my father death. they not told me say bye bye his life. After death of 6 June on 10 june my mom and dad anniversary.but my father is Best in the world they can do anything for me please take care of father and respect it of your parents.

CHAPTER ONE

Sachin Tendulkar Colour

- Sachin Tendulkar Colour

1. During writing this book no character & no religious are harmed written by Mr Vivek Kumar Pandey.

Sachin Ramesh Tendulkar was born 24 April 1973 is a former international cricketer of India who served as captain of the Indian national team. He is widely regarded as one of the greatest batsmen in the history of cricket. He is the highest run scorer of all time in international cricket, and the only player to have scored one hundred international centuries, the first batsman to score a double century in a One Day International (ODI), the holder of the record for the most runs in both Test and ODI cricket, and the only player to complete more than 30,000 runs in international cricket. In 2013, he was the only Indian cricketer included in an all-time Test World XI named to mark the 150th anniversary of Wisden Cricketers' Almanack. He is affectionately known as "Little Master" or "Master Blaster".

Tendulkar took up cricket at the age of eleven, made his Test debut on 15 November 1989 against Pakistan in Karachi at the age of sixteen, and went on to represent Mumbai domestically and India internationally for close to twenty-four years. In 2002, halfway through his career, Wisden Cricketers' Almanack ranked him the second-greatest Test batsman of all time, behind Don Bradman, and the second-greatest ODI batsman of all time, behind Viv Richards.Later in his career, Tendulkar was a part of the Indian team that won the 2011 World Cup, his first win in six World Cup appearances for India.He had previously been named "Player of the Tournament" at the 2003 edition of the tournament, held in South Africa.

Tendulkar received the Arjuna Award in 1994 for his outstanding sporting achievement, the Khel Ratna award in 1997, India's highest sporting honour, and the Padma Shri and Padma Vibhushan awards in 1999 and 2008, respectively, India's fourth- and second-highest civilian awards. After a few hours of his final match on 16 November 2013, the Prime Minister's Office announced the decision to award him the Bharat Ratna, India's highest civilian award. He is the youngest recipient to date and the first ever sportsperson to receive the award. He also won the 2010 Sir Garfield Sobers Trophy for cricketer of the year at the ICC awards. In 2012, Tendulkar was nominated to the Rajya Sabha, the upper house of the Parliament of India. He was also the first sportsperson and the first person without an aviation background to be awarded the honorary rank of group captain by the Indian Air Force. In 2012, he was named an Honorary Member of the Order of Australia.

In 2010, Time magazine included Sachin in its annual Time 100 list as one of the "Most Influential People in the World". In December 2012, Tendulkar announced his retirement from ODIs. He retired from Twenty20 cricket in October 2013 and subsequently retired from all forms of cricket on 16 November 2013 after playing his 200th Test match, against the West Indies in Mumbai's Wankhede Stadium. Tendulkar played 664 international cricket matches in total, scoring 34,357 runs.In 2019, Tendulkar was inducted into the ICC Cricket Hall of Fame.

- Early years

Tendulkar was born at Nirmal Nursing Home in Dadar, Bombay on 24 April 1973 to a Rajapur Saraswat Brahmin maharastrian famiy His father, Ramesh Tendulkar, was a well-known Marathi novelist & poet and his mother, Rajni, worked in the insurance industry.[38] Ramesh named Tendulkar after his favourite music director, Sachin Dev Burman. Tendulkar has three elder siblings: two half-brothers Nitin and Ajit, and a half-sister Savita. They were Ramesh's children by his first wife, who died after the birth of her third child.

Tendulkar spent his formative years in the Sahitya Sahawas Cooperative Housing Society in Bandra (East). As a young boy, Tendulkar was considered a bully, and often picked up fights with new children in his school.He also showed an interest in tennis, idolising John McEnroe. To help curb his mischievous and bullying tendencies, Ajit introduced the young

Sachin to cricket in 1984. He introduced him to Ramakant Achrekar, a famous cricket coach and a club cricketer of repute, at Shivaji Park, Dadar. In the first meeting, the young Sachin did not play his best. Ajit told Achrekar that he was feeling self-conscious due to the coach observing him, and was not displaying his natural game. Ajit requested the coach to give him another chance at playing, but watch while hiding behind a tree. This time, Sachin, apparently unobserved, played much better and was accepted at Achrekar's academy.

Achrekar was impressed with Tendulkar's talent and advised him to shift his schooling to Sharadashram Vidyamandir (English) High School, a school at Dadar which had a dominant cricket team and had produced many notable cricketers. Prior to this, Tendulkar had attended the Indian Education Society's New English School in Bandra (East). He was also coached under the guidance of Achrekar at Shivaji Park in the mornings and evenings. Tendulkar would practice for hours on end in the nets. If he became exhausted, Achrekar would put a one-rupee coin on the top of the stumps, and the bowler who dismissed Tendulkar would get the coin. If Tendulkar passed the whole session without getting dismissed, the coach would give him the coin. Tendulkar now considers the 13 coins he won then as some of his most prized possessions. He moved in with his aunt and uncle, who lived near Shivaji Park, during this period, due to his hectic schedule.

- Sachin Tendulkar and his wife Anjali

Meanwhile, at school, he developed a reputation as a child prodigy. He had become a common conversation point in local cricketing circles, where there were suggestions already that he would become one of the greats. Sachin consistently featured in the school team in the Matunga Gujarati Seva Mandal (MGSM) Shield. Besides school cricket, he also played club cricket, initially representing John Bright Cricket Club in Bombay's premier club cricket tournament, the Kanga League, and later went on to play for the Cricket Club of India. In 1987, at the age of 14, he attended the MRF Pace Foundation in Madras (now Chennai) to train as a fast bowler, but the Australian fast bowler Dennis Lillee, who took a world record 355 Test wickets, was unimpressed, suggesting that Tendulkar focus on his batting instead. On 20 January 1987, he also turned out as substitute for Imran Khan's side in an exhibition game at Brabourne Stadium in Bombay, to mark the golden jubilee of Cricket Club of India. A couple of months later, former Indian batsman Sunil Gavaskar gave him a pair of his own ultra light pads and consoled him to not get disheartened for not getting the Bombay Cricket Association's "Best junior cricket award" (He was 14 years that time). "It was the greatest source of encouragement for me," Tendulkar said nearly 20 years later after surpassing Gavaskar's world record of 34 Test centuries.Sachin served as a ball boy in the 1987 Cricket World Cup when India played against England in the semifinal in Bombay.

In his season in 1988, Tendulkar scored a century in every innings he played. He was involved in an unbroken 664-run partnership in a Lord Harris Shield inter-school game against St. Xavier's High School in 1988 with his friend and teammate Vinod Kambli, who would also go on to represent India. The destructive pair reduced one bowler to tears and made the rest of the opposition unwilling to continue the game. Tendulkar scored 326 (not out) in this innings and scored over a thousand runs in the tournament. This was a record partnership in any form of cricket until 2006, when it was broken by two under-13 batsmen in a match held at Hyderabad in India.

- Early domestic career

On 14 November 1987, the 14-year-old Tendulkar was selected to represent Bombay in the Ranji Trophy, India's premier domestic First-class cricket tournament, for the 1987–88 season. However, he was not selected for the final eleven in any of the matches, though he was often used as a substitute fielder. He narrowly missed out on playing alongside his idol Gavaskar, who had retired from all forms of cricket after the 1987 Cricket World Cup. A year later, on 11 December 1988, aged 15 years and 232 days, Tendulkar made his debut for Bombay against Gujarat at Wankhede stadium and scored 100 not out in that match, making him the youngest Indian to score a century on debut in first-class cricket. He was selected to play for the team by the then Bombay captain Dilip Vengsarkar after watching him easily playing India's best fast bowler at the time, Kapil Dev, in the Wankhede Stadium's Cricket practice nets,where the Indian team had come to play against the touring New Zealand team. He followed this by scoring a century in his first Deodhar and Duleep Trophies, which are also Indian domestic tournaments.

- Tendulkar finished the 1988–89 Ranji Trophy season as Bombay's highest run-scorer. He scored 583 runs at an average of 67.77, and was the eighth-highest run-scorer overall. In 1995- 96 Irani trophy he captained Mumbai against Rest of India team. He also made an unbeaten century in the Irani Trophy match against Delhi at the start of the 1989–90 season, playing for the Rest of India. Sachin was picked for a young Indian team to tour England twice, under the Star Cricket Club banner in 1988 and 1989.In the famous 1990–91 Ranji Trophy final, in which Haryana defeated Bombay by two runs after leading in the first innings, Tendulkar's 96 from 75 balls was a key to giving Bombay a chance of victory as it attempted to chase 355 from only 70 overs on the final day.

In the final of 1995 Ranji trophy, Tendulkar scored 140 and 139 versus Punjab at Wankhede playing as a captain. Against Haydrabad 53, 128 in 2000, 105, 43 against Bengal in 2007 are the innings he played for Mumbai in the final of Ranji trophy at Wankhede stadium.

His first double century (204*) was for Mumbai while playing against the visiting Australian team at the Brabourne Stadium in 1998. He is the only player to score a century on debut in all three of his domestic first-class tournaments (the Ranji, Irani, and Duleep Trophies).Another double century was an innings of 233* against Tamil Nadu in the semi-finals of the 2000 Ranji Trophy, which he regards as one of the best innings of his career.

- Yorkshire

In 1992, at the age of 19, Tendulkar became the first overseas-born player to represent Yorkshire, which prior to Tendulkar joining the team, never selected players even from outside Yorkshire. Selected for Yorkshire as a replacement for the injured Australian fast bowler Craig McDermott, Tendulkar played 16 first-class matches for the county and scored 1070 runs at an average of 46.52.

- International career

- Early career

Raj Singh Dungarpur is credited for the selection of Tendulkar for the Indian tour of Pakistan in late 1989, after one first class season.The Indian selection committee had shown interest in selecting Tendulkar for the tour of the West Indies held earlier that year, but eventually did not select him, as they did not want him to be exposed to the dominant fast bowlers of the West Indies so early in his career. Tendulkar made his Test debut against Pakistan in Karachi in November 1989 aged 16 years and 205 days. He made 15 runs, being bowled by Waqar Younis, who also made his debut in that match, but was noted for how he handled numerous blows to his body at the hands of the Pakistani pace attack.

In the fourth and final Test in Sialkot, he was hit on the nose by a bouncer bowled by Younis, but he declined medical assistance and continued to bat even as he gushed blood from it. In a 20-over exhibition game in Peshawar, held in parallel with the bilateral series, Tendulkar made 53 runs off 18 balls, including an over in which he scored 27 runs (6, 4, 0, 6, 6, 6) off leg-spinner Abdul Qadir. This was later called "one of the best innings I have seen" by the then Indian captain Krishnamachari Srikkanth. In all, he scored 215 runs at an average of 35.83 in the Test series, and was dismissed without scoring a run in the only One Day International (ODI) he played. Thus Sachin Tendulkar became the youngest player to debut for India in Tests at the age of 16 years and 205 days and also the youngest player to debut for India in ODIs at the age of 16 years and 238 days.

- The series was followed by a tour of New Zealand in which he scored 117 runs at an average of 29.25 in Tests including an innings of 88 in the second Test. He was dismissed without scoring in one of the two one-day games he played, and scored 36 in the other. On his next tour, a summer tour to England of 1990, on 14 August, he became the second youngest cricketer to score a Test century as he made 119 not out in the second Test at Old Trafford in Manchester, an innings which contributed to a draw and saved India from certain defeat in the match. Wisden described his innings as "a disciplined display of immense maturity" and also wrote.

He looked the embodiment of India's famous opener, Gavaskar, and indeed was wearing a pair of his pads. While he displayed a full repertoire of strokes in compiling his maiden Test hundred, most remarkable were his off-side shots from the back foot. Though only 5ft 5in tall, he was still able to control without difficulty short deliveries from the English pacemen.

Tendulkar further enhanced his reputation as a future great during the 1991–92 tour of Australia held before the 1992 Cricket World Cup, that included an unbeaten 148 in the third Test at Sydney, making him the youngest batsman to score a century in Australia. He then scored 114 on a fast, bouncing pitch in the final Test at Perth against a pace attack comprising Merv Hughes, Bruce Reid and Craig McDermott. Hughes commented to Allan Border at the time that "This little prick's going to get more runs than you, AB."

- Rise through the ranks

Tendulkar's performance through the years 1994–1999 coincided with his physical peak, in his early twenties. He opened the batting at Auckland against New Zealand in 1994, making 82 runs off 49 balls.He scored his first ODI century on 9 September 1994 against Australia in Sri Lanka at Colombo. It took him 78 ODIs to score his first century.

- Tendulkar waits at the bowler's end

Tendulkar's rise continued when he was the leading run scorer at the 1996 World Cup, scoring two centuries. He was the only Indian batsman to perform well in the semi-final against Sri Lanka. Tendulkar fell amid a batting collapse and the match referee, Clive Lloyd, awarded Sri Lanka the match after the crowd began rioting and throwing litter onto the field.

- After the World Cup, in the same year against Pakistan at Sharjah, Indian captain Mohammed Azharuddin was going through a lean patch. Tendulkar and Navjot Singh Sidhu both made centuries to set a then record partnership for the second wicket. After getting out, Tendulkar found Azharuddin in two minds about whether he should bat.Tendulkar convinced Azharuddin to bat and Azharuddin subsequently unleashed 24 runs off one over. India went on to win that match. It enabled India to post a score in excess of 300 runs for the first time in an ODI.

This was the beginning of a period at the top of the batting world, culminating in the Australian tour of India in early 1998, with Tendulkar scoring three consecutive centuries. The focus was on the clash between

Tendulkar, the world's most dominating batsman and Shane Warne, the world's leading spinner, both at the peak of their careers, clashing in a Test series. In the lead-up to the series, Tendulkar simulated scenarios in the nets with Laxman Sivaramakrishnan, the former India leg spinner, donning the role of Warne. In their tour opener, Australia faced the then Ranji Champions Mumbai at the Brabourne Stadium in a three-day first class match. Tendulkar made an unbeaten 204 as Shane Warne conceded 111 runs in 16 overs and Australia lost the match within three days.

He also had a role with the ball in the five-match ODI series in India following the Tests, including a five wicket haul in an ODI in Kochi. Set 310 runs to win, Australia were cruising at 203 for 3 in the 31st over when Tendulkar turned the match for India, taking the wickets of Michael Bevan, Steve Waugh, Darren Lehmann, Tom Moody and Damien Martyn for 32 runs in 10 overs.The Test match success was followed by two consecutive centuries in April 1998 in a Triangular cricket tournament in Sharjah—the first in a must-win game to take India to the finals and then again in the finals, both against Australia. These twin knocks were also known as the Desert Storm innings. Following the series, Warne ruefully joked that he was having nightmares about his Indian nemesis.

Tendulkar's contribution in the ICC 1998 quarterfinal at Dhaka paved the way for India's entry into the semifinals, when he took four Australian wickets after scoring 141 runs in 128 balls.

- The inaugural Asian Test Championship took place in February and March 1999, involving India, Pakistan, and Sri Lanka. In the first match, between India and Pakistan in Eden Gardens, Tendulkar was run out for nine after colliding with Pakistan bowler Shoaib Akhtar. Around 100,000 people came to support India during the initial four days of the tournament, breaking a 63-year-old record for aggregate Test attendance record.The crowd's reaction to Tendulkar's dismissal was to throw objects at Akhtar, and the players were taken off the field. The match resumed after Tendulkar and the president of the ICC appealed to the crowd; however, further rioting meant that the match was finished in front of a crowd of 200 people. Tendulkar scored his 19th Test century in the second Test and the match resulted in a draw with Sri Lanka. India did not progress to the final, which was won by Pakistan, and refused to participate the next time the championship was held due to increasing political tensions between India and Pakistan.

In the Test against Pakistan at Chepauk in 1999, the first of a two-Test series, Sachin scored 136 in the fourth innings with India chasing 271 for victory. However, he was out when India needed 17 more runs to win, triggering a batting collapse, and India lost the match by 12 runs. The worst was yet to come as Professor Ramesh Tendulkar, Sachin's father, died in the middle of the 1999 Cricket World Cup. Tendulkar flew back to India to attend the final rituals of his father, missing the match against Zimbabwe. However, he returned to the World Cup scoring a century (140 not out of 101 balls) in his very next match against Kenya in Bristol. He dedicated this century to his father.

- Tendulkar's record as captain

Tendulkar's two tenures as captain of the Indian cricket team were not very successful. When Tendulkar took over as captain in 1996, it was with huge hopes and expectations. However, by 1997 the team was performing poorly. Azharuddin was credited with saying "Nahin jeetega! Chote ki naseeb main jeet nahin hai!", which translates into: "He won't win! It's not in the small one's destiny!".

Tendulkar, succeeding Azharuddin as captain for his second term, led India on a tour of Australia, where the visitors were beaten 3–0 by the newly crowned world champions. Tendulkar, however, won the player of the series award as well as player of the match in one of the games. After another Test series defeat, this time by a 0–2 margin at home against South Africa, Tendulkar resigned, and Sourav Ganguly took over as captain in 2000.

During the Indian team's 2007 tour of England, the desire of Rahul Dravid to resign from the captaincy became known. The BCCI President Sharad Pawar offered the captaincy to Tendulkar, who instead recommended Mahendra Singh Dhoni to take over the reins. Pawar later revealed this conversation, crediting Tendulkar for first forwarding the name of Dhoni, who since achieved much success as captain.

- 2000 fixing matter

In the year of 2000 a huge match fixing scandal happened in Indian cricket. After the incident Sachin Tendulkar and other 3 senior cricketers played important role ensured that the players banned by BCCI and whose performance was dubious ware never picked for the Indian team again. Sachin and co. did this work quietly without doing public statements.

The continued calls for Tendulkar to be made captain, the offer of captaincy in 2007 and his rejection of the offer, there are numerous articles relating to where his faults were in captaincy.

- Mike Denness incident

In India's 2001 tour of South Africa in the second test match between India and South Africa at St George's Park, Port Elizabeth, match referee Mikc Denness fined four Indian players for excessive appealing, as well as fined the Indian captain Sourav Ganguly for not controlling his team.Tendulkar was given a suspended ban of one game by Denness in light of alleged ball tampering. Television cameras picked up images that suggested Tendulkar may have been involved in cleaning the seam of the cricket ball. This can, under some conditions, amount to altering the condition of the ball. Denness found Sachin Tendulkar guilty of ball tampering charges and handed him a one Test match ban. The incident escalated to include sports journalists accusing Denness of racism, and led to Denness being barred from entering the venue of the third Test match. The ICC revoked the status of the match as a Test as the teams rejected the appointed referee. The charges against Tendulkar and Sehwag's ban for excessive appealing triggered a massive backlash from the Indian public.

- Injuries and decline amid surpassing Bradman's haul

Sachin Tendulkar continued performing well in Test cricket in 2001 and 2002, with some pivotal performances with both bat and ball. Tendulkar took three wickets on the final day of the famous Kolkata Test against Australia in 2001, including the key wickets of Matthew Hayden and Adam Gilchrist, who were centurions in the previous Test. His three wickets haul helped India win the match. In the five-match ODI series that followed, he took his 100th wicket in ODIs, claiming the wicket of then Australian captain Steve Waugh in the final match at the Fatorda Stadium in Goa.

In the 2002 series in the West Indies, Tendulkar started well, scoring 79 in the first Test. In the second Test at Port of Spain, Sachin Tendulkar scored 117 in the first innings, his 29th Test century in his 93rd Test match, to equal Sir Donald Bradman's record of 29 Test hundreds. He was gifted a Ferrari

360 Modena by Fiat through Michael Schumacher for achieving this feat.

- Decline phase of career

Then, in a hitherto unprecedented sequence, he scored 0, 0, 8 and 0 in the next four innings.He returned to form in the last Test scoring 41 and 86, one half century. However, India lost the series. In this period, in the third Test match against England in August 2002, Sachin scored his 30th Test century to surpass Bradman's haul, in his 99th Test match.

- 2003 Cricket World Cup

Tendulkar made 673 runs in 11 matches in the 2003 Cricket World Cup, helping India reach the final. While Australia retained the trophy that they had won in 1999, Tendulkar was given the Man of the Tournament award.

He continued to score heavily in ODI cricket that year, with two hundreds in a tri-series involving New Zealand and Australia.As a part-time bowler, he dismissed an exhausted centurion, Matthew Hayden in the tri-series final.

- 2003 tour of Australia

The drawn series as India toured Australia in 2003–04 saw Tendulkar making his mark in the last Test of the series, scoring 241 not out from 436 balls with 33 fours at a strike rate of 55.27 in Sydney, putting India in a virtually unbeatable position. He spent 613 minutes at the crease during the innings. He followed this up with an unbeaten 60 in the second innings of the Test. Prior to this Test match, he had had an unusually horrible run of form, failing in all six innings in the preceding three Tests.It was no aberration that 2003 was his worst year in Test cricket, with an average of 17.00 and just one fifty.

Tendulkar scored an unbeaten 194 against Pakistan at Multan in the following series. Indian captain Rahul Dravid declared before Tendulkar reached 200; had he done so it would have been the fourth time he had passed the landmark in Tests. Tendulkar said that he was disappointed and that the declaration had taken him by surprise.Many former cricketers commented that Dravid's declaration was in bad taste.After the match, which India won, Dravid said that the matter had been discussed internally and put to rest.

A tennis elbow injury then took its toll on Tendulkar, leaving him out of the side for most of the year, coming back only for the last two Tests when Australia toured India in 2004.He played a part in India's victory in Mumbai in that series with a fast 55, though Australia took the series 2–1.

On 10 December 2005 at Feroz Shah Kotla, Tendulkar scored his record-breaking 35th Test century, against the Sri Lankans. After this, Tendulkar endured the longest spell of his career without a Test century: 17 innings elapsed before he scored 101 against Bangladesh in May 2007. Tendulkar scored his 39th ODI hundred on 6 February 2006 in a match against Pakistan. He followed with a 42 in the second One-Day International against Pakistan on 11 February 2006, and then a 95 in hostile, seaming conditions on 13 February 2006 in Lahore, which set up an Indian victory. On 19 March 2006, after being dismissed for only one run against England in the first innings of the third Test in his home ground, Wankhede, Tendulkar was booed off the ground by a section of the crowd, the first time that he had ever faced such flak. Tendulkar ended the three-Test series without a half-century to his credit, and the need for a shoulder operation raised more questions about his longevity.

Tendulkar's comeback came in the DLF cup in Malaysia and he was the only Indian batsman to shine. In his comeback match, against West Indies on 14 September 2006, Tendulkar responded to his critics who believed that his career was inexorably sliding with his 40th ODI century. Though he scored 141 not out, West Indies won the rain-affected match by the D/L method.

- 2007 Cricket World Cup debacle

During the preparation for the 2007 World Cup, Tendulkar's attitude was criticised by Indian team coach Greg Chappell. Chappell reportedly felt that Tendulkar would be more useful down the order, while the latter felt that he would be better off opening the innings, the role he had played for most of his career. Chappell also believed that Tendulkar's repeated failures were hurting the team's chances. In a rare show of emotion, Tendulkar hit out at the comments attributed to Chappell by pointing out that no coach had ever suggested his attitude towards cricket was incorrect. On 7 April 2007, the Board of Control for Cricket in India issued a notice to Tendulkar asking for an explanation for his comments made to the media. Chappell subsequently resigned as coach but said that this affair had no bearing on his decision and that he and Tendulkar were on good terms.

At the World Cup in the West Indies, Tendulkar and the Indian cricket team led by Rahul Dravid had a dismal campaign. Tendulkar, who was pushed to bat lower down the order had scores of 7 against Bangladesh, 57 not out against Bermuda and 0 against Sri Lanka. As a result, former Australian captain Ian Chappell, brother of Greg, called for Tendulkar to retire in his newspaper column.

After the loss against Bangladesh and Sri Lanka, Tendulkar was into depression and taught to retire from Cricket. But Viv Richards and Ajit Tendulkar stopped him. According to Sachin, 23 March 2007, the loss against minnows Bangladesh is one of the worst days of his cricketing career.

- Return to old form and consistency

In the subsequent Test series against Bangladesh, Tendulkar returned to his opening slot and was chosen as the Man of the Series. He continued by scoring 99 and 93 in the first two matches of the Future Cup against South Africa. During the second match, he also became the first to score 15,000 runs in ODIs. He was the leading run scorer and was adjudged the Man of the Series.

Tendulkar celebrates upon reaching his 38th Test century against Australia in the 2nd Test at the SCG in 2008, where he finished not out on 154

On the second day of the Nottingham Test on 28 July 2007, Tendulkar became the third cricketer to complete 11,000 Test runs. In the subsequent one-day series against England, Tendulkar was the leading run scorer from India with an average of 53.42. In the ODI Series against Australia in October 2007 Tendulkar was the leading Indian run scorer with 278 runs.

Tendulkar was dismissed five times in 2007 between 90 and 100, including three times at 99, leading some to suggestions that he struggles to cope with nervousness in this phase of his innings.Tendulkar has got out 27 times in the 90s during his international career. In a five-ODI series against Pakistan, he was caught by Kamran Akmal off the bowling of Umar Gul for 99 in the second match at Mohali, and in the fourth match of that series, he got out in the 90s for a second time, scoring 97 before dragging a delivery from Gul on to his stumps.

- 2007/08 tour of Australia

In the Border-Gavaskar Trophy, 2007–08, Tendulkar showed exceptional form, becoming the leading run scorer with 493 runs in four Tests, despite consistently failing in the second innings. Sachin scored 62 runs in the first innings of the first Test at the MCG in Melbourne, but could not prevent a heavy 337-run win for Australia. In the controversial New Years' Test at Sydney, Tendulkar scored an unbeaten 154, even though India lost the Test. This was his third century at the SCG and his 38th Test century overall, earning him an average of 326 at the ground at the time of completing the innings.

In the third Test at the WACA cricket ground in Perth, Sachin was instrumental in India's first innings score of 330, scoring a well-compiled 71. India went on to record a historic triumph at the WACA, ending Australia's run of 16 consecutive wins. In the fourth Test at the Adelaide Oval, which ended in a draw, he scored 153 in the first innings, being involved in a crucial 126-run stand with V.V.S. Laxman for the fifth wicket to lead India to a score of 282 for 5 from 156 for 4. He secured the Man of the Match award.

In the One-Day International Commonwealth Bank Tri-Series involving India, Sri Lanka and Australia, Tendulkar became the only batsman to complete 16,000 runs in ODIs.He achieved this feat against Sri Lanka on 5 February 2008 at the Gabba in Brisbane. He started the series wth scores of 10, 35, 44 and 32. His form dipped a bit in the middle of the tournament but Tendulkar came back strongly in India's must-win game against Sri Lanka at the Bellerive Oval in Hobart, scoring 63 off 54 balls.He finished the series with a match winning 117 not out off 120 balls in the first final, and 91 runs in the second final. Both the knocks were nominated to be the ODI Batting Performance of the year by ESPNCricinfo.

- Home series against South Africa

South Africa toured in March and April 2008 for a three-Test series. Tendulkar scored a five-ball duck in his only innings of the series he sustained a groin strain in the match and as a result was forced not only to miss the second and third Tests, but also the tri-series involving Bangladesh, the 2008 Asia Cup, and the first half of the inaugural season of the IPL.

- Sri Lanka series

Before the Indian cricket team's tour of Sri Lanka in July 2008, Tendulkar needed 177 runs to go past Brian Lara's record of Test 11,953 runs. However, he failed in all six innings, scoring a total of 95 runs. India lost the series and his average of 15.83 was his worst in a Test series with at least three matches.

- 2011 Cricket World Cup and after

From February to April, Bangladesh, India, and Sri Lanka hosted the 2011 World Cup. Amassing 482 runs at an average of 53.55 including two centuries, Tendulkar was India's leading run-scorer for the tournament; only Tillakaratne Dilshan of Sri Lanka scored more runs in the 2011 tournament, and was named in the ICC 'Team of the Tournament'. India defeated Sri Lanka in the final.Shortly after the victory, Tendulkar commented that "Winning the World Cup is the proudest moment of my life. ... I couldn't control my tears of joy."

- Tendulkar's results in international matches

India were due to tour the West Indies in June, although Tendulkar chose not to participate. He returned to the squad in July for India's tour of England. Throughout the tour there was much hype in the media about whether Tendulkar would reach his 100th century in international cricket (Test and ODIs combined). However, his highest score in the Tests was 91; Tendulkar averaged 34.12 in the series as England won 4–0 as they deposed India as the No. 1 ranked Test side.The injury Tendulkar sustained to his right foot in 2001 flared up and as a result he was ruled out of the ODI series that followed. Tendulkar created another record on 8 November 2011 when he became the first cricketer to score 15,000 runs in Test cricket, during the opening Test match against the West Indies at the Feroz Shah Kotla Stadium in New Delhi. For his performances in 2011, he was named in the World Test XI by the ICC.

Ian Chappell was not happy with Sachin's performance after India's tour of Australia. He says that Sachin's quest for his 100th hundred has proved to be a hurdle for the entire team and has hampered their performance on the Tour of Australia. Former India World Cup winning captain and all-rounder

Kapil Dev has also voiced his opinion that Sachin should have retired from ODI's after the World Cup. Former Australian fast bowler, Geoff Lawson, has said that Sachin has the right to decide when to quit although he adds that Tendulkar should not delay it for too long. The selection committee of BCCI expectedly included Sachin in the national Test squad for the upcoming series against New Zealand commencing in August 2012.

- 100th international century

Tendulkar scored his 100th international hundred on 16 March 2012, at Mirpur against Bangladesh in the Asia Cup. He became the first person in history to achieve this feat, which was also his first ODI hundred against Bangladesh. He said "It's been a tough phase for me ... I was not thinking about the milestone, the media started all this, wherever I went, the restaurant, room service, everyone was talking about the 100th hundred. Nobody talked about my 99 hundreds. It became mentally tough for me because nobody talked about my 99 hundreds." Despite Tendulkar's century, India failed to win the match against Bangladesh, losing by 5 wickets.

- Return to Ranji Trophy

After being bowled out in three similar instances against New Zealand and hitting a slump in form, Tendulkar returned to the Ranji Trophy to get back some form ahead of the England Series at home, in a match for Mumbai against Railways on 2 November 2012. This was his first Ranji Trophy match since 2009. He scored 137 off 136 balls, with 21 fours and 3 sixes, to take his team to 344 for 4 at stumps on day one.

However, because of a poor form in the first two Tests in the series against England, and India being humiliated in the second match of that series by 10 wickets on 26 November 2012,some people have started to question his place in the Indian team. A report by The Hindustan Times said that Tendulkar had a discussion with the national chief selector Sandeep Patil, in which he said that he would leave it to the selectors to decide on his future as he is not getting any runs. This speculation, however, was later considered to be false.

Then he decided to play in the knockout stage of the 2012–13 Ranji Trophy. He scored 108 in the quarter final against Baroda before being bowled by Murtuja Vahora, where Sachin was involved in a 234-run partnership with opener Wasim Jaffer (150) for the 3rd wicket at Wankhede Stadium. Mumbai eventually piled on 645/9 and won on 1st innings lead. In the semi final against Services at Palam A Ground, with Mumbai reeling at 23/3, Sachin scored 56 from 75 balls and had an 81-run 4th wicket partnership with Abhishek Nayar (70), and Mumbai eventually won on 1st innings lead after the match went into the sixth day due to rain delays. In the final against Saurashtra, he was run out for 22 following a misunderstanding with Wasim Jaffer. Mumbai eventually won the Ranji Trophy 2012–13.

He also played in the Irani Trophy for Mumbai, where he scored 140* against Rest of India and helped Mumbai to score 409 in reply to Rest of India's 526. This was also his 81st hundred in first-class cricket, equalling Sunil Gavaskar's Indian record for most first-class hundreds.

- Retirement

Following poor performance in the 2012 series against England, Tendulkar announced his retirement from One Day Internationals on 23 December 2012, while noting that he will be available for Test cricket. In response to the news, former India captain Sourav Ganguly noted that Tendulkar could have played the up-coming series against Pakistan, while Anil Kumble said it would be "tough to see an Indian (ODI) team list without Tendulkar's name in it", and Javagal Srinath mentioned that Tendulkar "changed the way ODIs were played right from the time he opened in New Zealand in 1994".

After playing a Twenty20 International in 2006 against South Africa, he said that he would not play the format again.He announced his retirement from the IPL after his team, Mumbai Indians, beat Chennai Super Kings by 23 runs at the Eden Gardens in Kolkata on 26 May to win the Indian Premier League 2013. He retired from Twenty20 cricket and limited-overs cricket, after playing the 2013 Champions League Twenty20 in September–October 2013 in India for Mumbai Indians.

On 10 October 2013 Tendulkar announced that he would retire from all cricket after the two-Test series against West Indies in November. At his request, the BCCI arranged that the two matches be played at Kolkata and Mumbai so that the farewell would happen at his home ground. He scored 74 runs in his last Test innings against West Indies, thus failing short by 79 runs to complete 16,000 runs in Test cricket, the next man to bat after him was the future captain Virat Kohli. The Cricket Association of Bengal and the Mumbai Cricket Association organised events to mark his retirement from the sport. Various national and international figures from cricket, politics, Bollywood and other fields spoke about him in a day-long Salaam Sachin Conclave organised by India Today.

- National honours

1. 1994 – Arjuna Award, by the Government of India in recognition of his outstanding achievement in sports.
2. 1997–98 – Rajiv Gandhi Khel Ratna, India's highest honour given for achievement in sports.
3. 1999 – Padma Shri, India's fourth-highest civilian award.
4. 2001 – Maharashtra Bhushan Award, Maharashtra State's highest Civilian Award.
5. 2008 – Padma Vibhushan, India's second-highest civilian award.
6. 2014 – Bharat Ratna, India's highest civilian award.

- Other honours

1. 2013 postage stamps commemorating the Sachin Tendulkar 200th Test Match
2. 1997 – Wisden Cricketer of the Year
3. 1998, 2010 – Wisden Leading Cricketer in the World
4. 2001 - Mumbai Cricket Association renamed Wankhede stadium's a stand after Sachin Tendulkar
5. 2002 – In commemorating Tendulkar's feat of equalling Don Bradman's 29 centuries in Test Cricket, automotive company Ferrari invited him to its paddock in Silverstone on the eve of the British Grand Prix on 23 July, to receive a Ferrari 360 Modena from the F1 world champion Michael Schumacher
6. 2003 – Player of the tournament in 2003 Cricket World Cup
7. 2004, 2007, 2010 – ICC World ODI XI
8. 2006-07, 2009-10 - Polly Umrigar Award for International cricketer of the year
9. 2009, 2010, 2011 – ICC World Test XI
10. 2010 – Outstanding Achievement in Sport and the Peoples Choice Award at The Asian Awards in London.

11. 2010 – Sir Garfield Sobers Trophy for cricketer of the year
12. 2010 – LG People's Choice Award
13. 2010 – Made an Honorary group captain by the Indian Air Force
14. 2011 – Castrol Indian Cricketer of the Year award
15. 2012 – Wisden India Outstanding Achievement award
16. 2012 – Honorary Member of the Order of Australia, given by the Australian government
17. 2013 – Indian Postal Service released a stamp of Tendulkar and he became the second Indian after Mother Teresa to have such stamp released in their lifetime
18. 2014 – ESPNCricinfo Cricketer of the Generation
19. 2017 – The Asian Awards Fellowship Award at the 7th Asian Awards
20. 2019 – Inducted into the ICC Cricket Hall of Fame
21. 2020 – Laureus World Sports Award for Best Sporting Moment (2000–2020)

Let's Know About Cricket

- Cricket

Cricket is a bat-and-ball game played between two teams of eleven players on a field at the centre of which is a 22-yard (20-metre) pitch with a wicket at each end, each comprising two bails balanced on three stumps. The game proceeds when a player on the fielding team, called the bowler, "bowls" (propels) the ball from one end of the pitch towards the wicket at the other end. The batting side's players score runs by striking the bowled ball with a bat and running between the wickets, while the bowling side tries to prevent this by keeping the ball within the field and getting it to either wicket, and dismiss each batter (so they are "out"). Means of dismissal include being bowled, when the ball hits the stumps and dislodges the bails, and by the fielding side either catching a hit ball before it touches the ground, or hitting a wicket with the ball before a batter can cross the crease line in front of the wicket to complete a run. When ten batters have been dismissed, the innings ends and the teams swap roles. The game is adjudicated by two umpires, aided by a third umpire and match referee in international matches.

Forms of cricket range from Twenty20, with each team batting for a single innings of 20 overs and the game generally lasting three hours, to Test matches played over five days. Traditionally cricketers play in all-white kit, but in limited overs cricket they wear club or team colours. In addition to the basic kit, some players wear protective gear to prevent injury caused by the ball, which is a hard, solid spheroid made of compressed leather with a slightly raised sewn seam enclosing a cork core layered with tightly wound string.

The earliest reference to cricket is in South East England in the mid-16th century. It spread globally with the expansion of the British Empire, with the first international matches in the second half of the 19th century. The game's governing body is the International Cricket Council (ICC), which has over 100 members, twelve of which are full members who play Test matches. The game's rules, the Laws of Cricket, are maintained by Marylebone Cricket Club (MCC) in London. The sport is followed primarily in South Asia, Australasia, the United Kingdom, southern Africa and the West Indies.Women's cricket, which is organised and played separately, has also achieved international standard. The most successful side playing international cricket is Australia, which has won seven One Day International trophies, including five World Cups, more than any other country and has been the top-rated Test side more than any other country.

- History of cricket to 1725

A medieval "club ball" game involving an underhand bowl towards a batter. Ball catchers are shown positioning themselves to catch a ball. Detail from the Canticles of Holy Mary, 13th century.

Cricket is one of many games in the "club ball" sphere that basically involve hitting a ball with a hand-held implement; others include baseball (which shares many similarities with cricket, both belonging in the more specific bat-and-ball games category), golf, hockey, tennis, squash, badminton and table tennis. In cricket's case, a key difference is the existence of a solid target structure, the wicket (originally, it is thought, a "wicket gate" through which sheep were herded), that the batter must defend. The cricket historian Harry Altham identified three "groups" of "club ball" games: the "hockey group", in which the ball is driven to and fro between two targets (the goals); the "golf group", in which the ball is driven towards an undefended target (the hole); and the "cricket group", in which "the ball is aimed at a mark (the wicket) and driven away from it".

It is generally believed that cricket originated as a children's game in the south-eastern counties of England, sometime during the medieval period.Although there are claims for prior dates, the earliest definite reference to cricket being played comes from evidence given at a court case in Guildford in January 1597 (Old Style), equating to January 1598 in the modern calendar. The case concerned ownership of a certain plot of land and the court heard the testimony of a 59-year-old coroner, John Derrick, who gave witness that.

Being a scholler in the ffree schoole of Guldeford hee and diverse of his fellows did runne and play there at creckett and other plaies.

Given Derrick's age, it was about half a century earlier when he was at school and so it is certain that cricket was being played c. 1550 by boys in Surrey. The view that it was originally a children's game is reinforced by Randle Cotgrave's 1611 English-French dictionary in which he defined the noun "crosse" as "the crooked staff wherewith boys play at cricket" and the verb form "crosser" as "to play at cricket".

One possible source for the sport's name is the Old English word "cryce" (or "cricc") meaning a crutch or staff. In Samuel Johnson's Dictionary, he derived cricket from "cryce, Saxon, a stick". In Old French, the word "criquet" seems to have meant a kind of club or stick. Given the strong medieval trade connections between south-east England and the County of Flanders when the latter belonged to the Duchy of Burgundy, the name may have been derived from the Middle Dutch (in use in Flanders at the time) "krick"(-e), meaning a stick (crook). Another possible source is the Middle Dutch word "krickstoel", meaning a long low stool used for kneeling in church and which resembled the long low wicket with two stumps used in early cricket. According to Heiner Gillmeister, a European language expert of Bonn University, "cricket" derives from the Middle Dutch phrase for hockey, met de (krik ket)sen (i.e., "with the stick chase"). Gillmeister has suggested that not only the name but also the sport itself may be of Flemish origin.

- Growth of amateur and professional cricket in England

Evolution of the cricket bat. The original "hockey stick" (left) evolved into the straight bat from c. 1760 when pitched delivery bowling began.

Although the main object of the game has always been to score the most runs, the early form of cricket differed from the modern game in certain key technical aspects; the North American variant of cricket known as wicket retained many of these aspects. The ball was bowled underarm by the bowler and along the ground towards a batter armed with a bat that in shape resembled a hockey stick; the batter defended a low, two-stump wicket; and runs were called notches because the scorers recorded them by notching tally sticks.

In 1611, the year Cotgrave's dictionary was published, ecclesiastical court records at Sidlesham in Sussex state that two parishioners, Bartholomew Wyatt and Richard Latter, failed to attend church on Easter Sunday because they were playing cricket. They were fined 12d each and ordered to do penance.This is the earliest mention of adult participation in cricket and it was around the same time that the earliest known organised inter-parish or village match was played – at Chevening, Kent. In 1624, a player called Jasper Vinall died after he was accidentally struck on the head during a match between two parish teams in Sussex.

Cricket remained a low-key local pursuit for much of the 17th century. It is known, through numerous references found in the records of ecclesiastical court cases, to have been proscribed at times by the Puritans before and during the Commonwealth. The problem was nearly always the issue of Sunday play as the Puritans considered cricket to be "profane" if played on the Sabbath, especially if large crowds or gambling were involved.

According to the social historian Derek Birley, there was a "great upsurge of sport after the Restoration" in 1660. Gambling on sport became a problem significant enough for Parliament to pass the 1664 Gambling Act, limiting stakes to £100 which was, in any case, a colossal sum exceeding the annual income of 99% of the population. Along with prizefighting, horse racing and blood sports, cricket was perceived to be a gambling sport.Rich patrons made matches for high stakes, forming teams in which they engaged the first professional players.By the end of the century, cricket had developed into a major sport that was spreading throughout England and was already being taken abroad by English mariners and colonisers – the earliest reference to cricket overseas is dated 1676. A 1697 newspaper report survives of "a great cricket match" played in Sussex "for fifty guineas apiece" – this is the earliest known contest that is generally considered a First Class match.

- The patrons, and other players from the social class known as the "gentry", began to classify themselves as "amateurs" to establish a clear distinction from the professionals, who were invariably members of the working class, even to the point of having separate changing and dining facilities. The gentry, including such high-ranking nobles as the Dukes of Richmond, exerted their honour code of noblesse oblige to claim rights of leadership in any sporting contests they took part in, especially as it was necessary for them to play alongside their "social inferiors" if they were to win their bets. In time, a perception took hold that the typical amateur who played in first-class cricket, until 1962 when amateurism was abolished, was someone with a public school education who had then gone to one of Cambridge or Oxford University – society insisted that such people were "officers and gentlemen" whose destiny was to provide leadership. In a purely financial sense, the cricketing amateur would theoretically claim expenses for playing while his professional counterpart played under contract and was paid a wage or match fee; in practice, many amateurs claimed more than actual expenditure and the derisive term "shamateur" was coined to describe the practice.

- The Young Cricketer, 1768

The game underwent major development in the 18th century to become England's national sport.Its success was underwritten by the twin necessities of patronage and betting. Cricket was prominent in London as early as 1707 and, in the middle years of the century, large crowds flocked to matches on the Artillery Ground in Finsbury. The single wicket form of the sport attracted huge crowds and wagers to match, its popularity peaking in the 1748 season. Bowling underwent an evolution around 1760 when bowlers began to pitch the ball instead of rolling or skimming it towards the batter. This caused a revolution in bat design because, to deal with the bouncing ball, it was necessary to introduce the modern straight bat in place of the old "hockey stick" shape.

The Hambledon Club was founded in the 1760s and, for the next twenty years until the formation of Marylebone Cricket Club (MCC) and the opening of Lord's Old Ground in 1787, Hambledon was both the game's greatest club and its focal point. MCC quickly became the sport's premier club and the custodian of the Laws of Cricket. New Laws introduced in the latter part of the 18th century included the three stump wicket and leg before wicket (lbw).

The 19th century saw underarm bowling superseded by first roundarm and then overarm bowling. Both developments were controversial.Organisation of the game at county level led to the creation of the county clubs, starting with Sussex in 1839. In December 1889, the eight leading county clubs formed the official County Championship, which began in 1890.

The most famous player of the 19th century was W. G. Grace, who started his long and influential career in 1865. It was especially during the career of Grace that the distinction between amateurs and professionals became blurred by the existence of players like him who were nominally amateur but, in terms of their financial gain, de facto professional. Grace himself was said to have been paid more money for playing cricket than any professional.

The last two decades before the First World War have been called the "Golden Age of cricket". It is a nostalgic name prompted by the collective sense of loss resulting from the war, but the period did produce some great players and memorable matches, especially as organised competition at county and Test level developed.

- Cricket becomes an international sport

In 1844, the first-ever international match took place between the United States and Canada. In 1859, a team of English players went to North America on the first overseas tour. Meanwhile, the British Empire had been instrumental in spreading the game overseas and by the middle of the 19th century it had become well established in Australia, the Caribbean, India, Pakistan, New Zealand, North America and South Africa.

In 1862, an English team made the first tour of Australia. The first Australian team to travel overseas consisted of Aboriginal stockmen who toured England in 1868. The first One Day International match was played on 5 January 1971 between Australia and England at the Melbourne Cricket Ground.

In 1876–77, an England team took part in what was retrospectively recognised as the first-ever Test match at the Melbourne Cricket Ground against Australia. The rivalry between England and Australia gave birth to The Ashes in 1882, and this has remained Test cricket's most famous contest. Test cricket began to expand in 1888–89 when South Africa played England.

- World cricket in the 20th century

The inter-war years were dominated by Australia's Don Bradman, statistically the greatest Test batter of all time. Test cricket continued to expand during the 20th century with the addition of the West Indies (1928),

New Zealand (1930) and India (1932) before the Second World War and then Pakistan (1952), Sri Lanka (1982), Zimbabwe (1992), Bangladesh (2000), Ireland and Afghanistan (both 2018) in the post-war period. South Africa was banned from international cricket from 1970 to 1992 as part of the apartheid boycott.

- The rise of limited overs cricket

Cricket entered a new era in 1963 when English counties introduced the limited overs variant. As it was sure to produce a result, limited overs cricket was lucrative and the number of matches increased. The first Limited Overs International was played in 1971 and the governing International Cricket Council (ICC), seeing its potential, staged the first limited overs Cricket World Cup in 1975. In the 21st century, a new limited overs form, Twenty20, made an immediate impact. On 22 June 2017, Afghanistan and Ireland became the 11th and 12th ICC full members, enabling them to play Test cricket.

- A typical cricket field.

In cricket, the rules of the game are specified in a code called The Laws of Cricket (hereinafter called "the Laws") which has a global remit. There are 42 Laws (always written with a capital "L"). The earliest known version of the code was drafted in 1744 and, since 1788, it has been owned and maintained by its custodian, the Marylebone Cricket Club (MCC) in London.

- Playing area

Cricket is a bat-and-ball game played on a cricket field between two teams of eleven players each. The field is usually circular or oval in shape and the edge of the playing area is marked by a boundary, which may be a fence, part of the stands, a rope, a painted line or a combination of these; the boundary must if possible be marked along its entire length.

In the approximate centre of the field is a rectangular pitch (see image, below) on which a wooden target called a wicket is sited at each end; the wickets are placed 22 yards (20 m) apart. The pitch is a flat surface 10 feet (3.0 m) wide, with very short grass that tends to be worn away as the game progresses (cricket can also be played on artificial surfaces, notably matting). Each wicket is made of three wooden stumps topped by two bails.

- Cricket pitch and creases

As illustrated above, the pitch is marked at each end with four white painted lines: a bowling crease, a popping crease and two return creases. The three stumps are aligned centrally on the bowling crease, which is eight feet eight inches long. The popping crease is drawn four feet in front of the bowling crease and parallel to it; although it is drawn as a twelve-foot line (six feet either side of the wicket), it is, in fact, unlimited in length. The return creases are drawn at right angles to the popping crease so that they intersect the ends of the bowling crease; each return crease is drawn as an eight-foot line, so that it extends four feet behind the bowling crease, but is also, in fact, unlimited in length.

Before a match begins, the team captains (who are also players) toss a coin to decide which team will bat first and so take the first innings. Innings is the term used for each phase of play in the match.In each innings, one team bats, attempting to score runs, while the other team bowls and fields the ball, attempting to restrict the scoring and dismiss the batters. When the first innings ends, the teams change roles; there can be two to four innings depending upon the type of match. A match with four scheduled innings is played over three to five days; a match with two scheduled innings is usually completed in a single day. During an innings, all eleven members of the fielding team take the field, but usually only two members of the batting team are on the field at any given time. The exception to this is if a batter has any type of illness or injury restricting his or her ability to run, in this case the batter is allowed a runner who can run between the wickets when the batter hits a scoring run or runs,though this does not apply in international cricket. The order of batters is usually announced just before the match, but it can be varied.

The main objective of each team is to score more runs than their opponents but, in some forms of cricket, it is also necessary to dismiss all of the opposition batters in their final innings in order to win the match, which would otherwise be drawn. If the team batting last is all out having scored fewer runs than their opponents, they are said to have "lost by n runs" (where n is the difference between the aggregate number of runs scored by the teams). If the team that bats last scores enough runs to win, it is said to have "won by n wickets", where n is the number of wickets left to fall. For example, a team that passes its opponents' total having lost six wickets (i.e., six of their batters have been dismissed) have won the match "by four wickets".

In a two-innings-a-side match, one team's combined first and second innings total may be less than the other side's first innings total. The team with the greater score is then said to have "won by an innings and n runs", and does not need to bat again: n is the difference between the two teams' aggregate scores. If the team batting last is all out, and both sides have scored the same number of runs, then the match is a tie; this result is quite rare in matches of two innings a side with only 62 happening in first-class matches from the earliest known instance in 1741 until January 2017. In the traditional form of the game, if the time allotted for the match expires before either side can win, then the game is declared a draw.

If the match has only a single innings per side, then a maximum number of overs applies to each innings. Such a match is called a "limited overs" or "one-day" match, and the side scoring more runs wins regardless of the number of wickets lost, so that a draw cannot occur. In some cases, ties are broken by having each team bat for a one-over innings known as a Super Over; subsequent Super Overs may be played if the first Super Over ends in a tie. If this kind of match is temporarily interrupted by bad weather, then a complex mathematical formula, known as the Duckworth–Lewis–Stern method after its developers, is often used to recalculate a new target score. A one-day match can also be declared a "no-result" if fewer than a previously agreed number of overs have been bowled by either team, in circumstances that make normal resumption of play impossible; for example, wet weather.

In all forms of cricket, the umpires can abandon the match if bad light or rain makes it impossible to continue. There have been instances of entire matches, even Test matches scheduled to be played over five days, being lost to bad weather without a ball being bowled: for example, the third Test of the 1970/71 series in Australia.

• Innings

The innings (ending with 's' in both singular and plural form) is the term used for each phase of play during a match. Depending on the type of match being played, each team has either one or two innings. Sometimes all eleven members of the batting side take a turn to bat but, for various reasons, an innings can end before they have all done so. The innings terminates if the batting team is "all out", a term defined by the Laws: "at the fall of a wicket or the retirement of a batter, further balls remain to be bowled but no further batter is available to come in". In this situation, one of the batters has not been dismissed and is termed not out; this is because he has no partners left and there must always be two active batters while the innings is in progress.

- An innings may end early while there are still two not out batters

the batting team's captain may declare the innings closed even though some of his players have not had a turn to bat: this is a tactical decision by the captain, usually because he believes his team have scored sufficient runs and need time to dismiss the opposition in their innings

the set number of overs (i.e., in a limited overs match) have been bowled

the match has ended prematurely due to bad weather or running out of time

in the final innings of the match, the batting side has reached its target and won the game.

- Overs

The Laws state that, throughout an innings, "the ball shall be bowled from each end alternately in overs of 6 balls". The name "over" came about because the umpire calls "Over!" when six balls have been bowled. At this point, another bowler is deployed at the other end, and the fielding side changes ends while the batters do not. A bowler cannot bowl two successive overs, although a bowler can (and usually does) bowl alternate overs, from the same end, for several overs which are termed a "spell". The batters do not change ends at the end of the over, and so the one who was non-striker is now the striker and vice versa. The umpires also change positions so that the one who was at "square leg" now stands behind the wicket at the non-striker's end and vice versa.

- Clothing and equipment

English cricketer W. G. Grace "taking guard" in 1883. His pads and bat are very similar to those used today. The gloves have evolved somewhat. Many modern players use more defensive equipment than were available to Grace, most notably helmets and arm guards.

The wicket-keeper (a specialised fielder behind the batter) and the batters wear protective gear because of the hardness of the ball, which can be delivered at speeds of more than 145 kilometres per hour (90 mph) and presents a major health and safety concern. Protective clothing includes pads (designed to protect the knees and shins), batting gloves or wicket-keeper's gloves for the hands, a safety helmet for the head and a box for male players inside the trousers (to protect the crotch area). Some batters wear additional padding inside their shirts and trousers such as thigh pads, arm pads, rib protectors and shoulder pads. The only fielders allowed to wear protective gear are those in positions very close to the batter (i.e., if they are alongside or in front of him), but they cannot wear gloves or external leg guards.

Subject to certain variations, on-field clothing generally includes a collared shirt with short or long sleeves; long trousers; woolen pullover (if needed); cricket cap (for fielding) or a safety helmet; and spiked shoes or boots to increase traction. The kit is traditionally all white and this remains the case in Test and first-class cricket but, in limited overs cricket, team colours are worn instead.

- Bat and ball

Two types of cricket ball, both of the same size:
i) A used white ball. White balls are mainly used in limited overs cricket, especially in matches played at night, under floodlights (left).
ii) A used red ball. Red balls are used in Test cricket, first-class cricket and some other forms of cricket (right).
The essence of the sport is that a bowler delivers (i.e., bowls) the ball from his or her end of the pitch towards the batter who, armed with a bat, is "on strike" at the other end (see next sub-section: Basic gameplay).
The bat is made of wood, usually Salix alba (white willow), and has the shape of a blade topped by a cylindrical handle. The blade must not be more than 4.25 inches (10.8 cm) wide and the total length of the bat not more than 38 inches (97 cm). There is no standard for the weight, which is usually between 2 lb 7 oz and 3 lb (1.1 and 1.4 kg).

The ball is a hard leather-seamed spheroid, with a circumference of 9 inches (23 cm). The ball has a "seam": six rows of stitches attaching the leather shell of the ball to the string and cork interior. The seam on a new ball is prominent and helps the bowler propel it in a less predictable manner. During matches, the quality of the ball deteriorates to a point where it is no longer usable; during the course of this deterioration, its behaviour in flight will change and can influence the outcome of the match. Players will, therefore, attempt to modify the ball's behaviour by modifying its physical properties. Polishing the ball and wetting it with sweat or saliva is legal, even when the polishing is deliberately done on one side only to increase the ball's swing through the air, but the acts of rubbing other substances into the ball, scratching the surface or picking at the seam are illegal ball tampering.

- Player roles

Basic gameplay: bowler to batter
During normal play, thirteen players and two umpires are on the field. Two of the players are batters and the rest are all eleven members of the fielding team. The other nine players in the batting team are off the field in the pavilion. The image with overlay below shows what is happening when a ball is being bowled and which of the personnel are on or close to the pitch.

- Return crease

In the photo, the two batters (3 & 8; wearing yellow) have taken position at each end of the pitch (6). Three members of the fielding team (4, 10 & 11; wearing dark blue) are in shot. One of the two umpires (1; wearing white hat) is stationed behind the wicket (2) at the bowler's (4) end of the pitch. The bowler (4) is bowling the ball (5) from his end of the pitch to the batter at the other end who is called the "striker". The other batter (3) at the bowling end is called the "non-striker". The wicket-keeper (10), who is a specialist, is positioned behind the striker's wicket (9) and behind him stands one of the fielders in a position called "first slip" (11). While the bowler and the first slip are wearing conventional kit only, the two batters and the wicket-keeper are wearing protective gear including safety helmets, padded gloves and leg guards (pads).

While the umpire (1) in shot stands at the bowler's end of the pitch, his colleague stands in the outfield, usually in or near the fielding position called "square leg", so that he is in line with the popping crease (7) at the striker's end of the pitch. The bowling crease (not numbered) is the one on which the wicket is located between the return creases (12). The bowler (4) intends to hit the wicket (9) with the ball (5) or, at least, to prevent the striker (8) from scoring runs. The striker (8) intends, by using his bat, to defend his wicket and, if possible, to hit the ball away from the pitch in order to score runs.

Some players are skilled in both batting and bowling, or as either or these as well as wicket-keeping, so are termed all-rounders. Bowlers are classified according to their style, generally as fast bowlers, seam bowlers or spinners. Batters are classified according to whether they are right-handed or left-handed.

• Fielding

Of the eleven fielders, three are in shot in the image above. The other eight are elsewhere on the field, their positions determined on a tactical basis by the captain or the bowler. Fielders often change position between deliveries, again as directed by the captain or bowler.

If a fielder is injured or becomes ill during a match, a substitute is allowed to field instead of him, but the substitute cannot bowl or act as a captain, except in the case of concussion substitutes in international cricket. The substitute leaves the field when the injured player is fit to return. The Laws of Cricket were updated in 2017 to allow substitutes to act as wicket-keepers.

• Bowling and dismissal

Glenn McGrath of Australia holds the world record for most wickets in the Cricket World Cup.

Most bowlers are considered specialists in that they are selected for the team because of their skill as a bowler, although some are all-rounders and even specialist batters bowl occasionally. The specialists bowl several times during an innings but may not bowl two overs consecutively. If the captain wants a bowler to "change ends", another bowler must temporarily fill in so that the change is not immediate.

A bowler reaches his delivery stride by means of a "run-up" and an over is deemed to have begun when the bowler starts his run-up for the first delivery of that over, the ball then being "in play".

Fast bowlers, needing momentum, take a lengthy run up while bowlers with a slow delivery take no more than a couple of steps before bowling. The fastest bowlers can deliver the ball at a speed of over 145 kilometres per hour (90 mph) and they sometimes rely on sheer speed to try to defeat the batter, who is forced to react very quickly.

Other fast bowlers rely on a mixture of speed and guile by making the ball seam or swing (i.e. curve) in flight. This type of delivery can deceive a batter into miscuing his shot, for example, so that the ball just touches the edge of the bat and can then be "caught behind" by the wicket-keeper or a slip fielder. At the other end of the bowling scale is the spin bowler who bowls at a relatively slow pace and relies entirely on guile to deceive the batter. A spinner will often "buy his wicket" by "tossing one up" (in a slower, steeper parabolic path) to lure the batter into making a poor shot. The batter has to be very wary of such deliveries as they are often "flighted" or spun so that the ball will not behave quite as he expects and he could be "trapped" into getting himself out. In between the pacemen and the spinners are the medium paced seamers who rely on persistent accuracy to try to contain the rate of scoring and wear down the batter's concentration.

There are nine ways in which a batter can be dismissed: five relatively common and four extremely rare. The common forms of dismissal are bowled, caught, leg before wicket (lbw), run out and stumped. Rare methods are hit wicket,hit the ball twice, obstructing the field and timed out. The Laws state that the fielding team, usually the bowler in practice, must appeal for a dismissal before the umpire can give his decision. If the batter is out, the umpire raises a forefinger and says "Out!"; otherwise, he will shake his head and say "Not out".There is, effectively, a tenth method of dismissal, retired out, which is not an on-field dismissal as such but rather a retrospective one for which no fielder is credited.

• Batting, runs and extras

The directions in which a right-handed batter, facing down the page, intends to send the ball when playing various cricketing shots. The diagram for a left-handed batter is a mirror image of this one.

Batters take turns to bat via a batting order which is decided beforehand by the team captain and presented to the umpires, though the order remains flexible when the captain officially nominates the team. Substitute batters are generally not allowed, except in the case of concussion substitutes in international cricket.

In order to begin batting the batter first adopts a batting stance. Standardly, this involves adopting a slight crouch with the feet pointing across the front of the wicket, looking in the direction of the bowler, and holding the bat so it passes over the feet and so its tip can rest on the ground near to the toes of the back foot.

A skilled batter can use a wide array of "shots" or "strokes" in both defensive and attacking mode. The idea is to hit the ball to the best effect with the flat surface of the bat's blade. If the ball touches the side of the bat it is called an "edge". The batter does not have to play a shot and can allow the ball to go through to the wicketkeeper. Equally, he does not have to attempt a run when he hits the ball with his bat. Batters do not always seek to hit the ball as hard as possible, and a good player can score runs just by making a deft stroke with a turn of the wrists or by simply "blocking" the ball but directing it away from fielders so that he has time to take a run. A wide variety of shots are played, the batter's repertoire including strokes named according to the style of swing and the direction aimed: e.g., "cut", "drive", "hook", "pull".

The batter on strike (i.e. the "striker") must prevent the ball hitting the wicket, and try to score runs by hitting the ball with his bat so that he and his partner have time to run from one end of the pitch to the other before the fielding side can return the ball. To register a run, both runners must touch the ground behind the popping crease with either their bats or their bodies (the batters carry their bats as they run). Each completed run increments the score of both the team and the striker.

- Sachin Tendulkar is the only player to have scored one hundred international centuries

The decision to attempt a run is ideally made by the batter who has the better view of the ball's progress, and this is communicated by calling: usually "yes", "no" or "wait". More than one run can be scored from a single hit: hits worth one to three runs are common, but the size of the field is such that it is usually difficult to run four or more. To compensate for this, hits that reach the boundary of the field are automatically awarded four runs if the ball touches the ground en route to the boundary or six runs if the ball clears the boundary without touching the ground within the boundary. In these cases the batters do not need to run. Hits for five are unusual and generally rely on the help of "overthrows" by a fielder returning the ball. If an odd number of runs is scored by the striker, the two batters have changed ends, and the one who was non-striker is now the striker. Only the striker can score individual runs, but all runs are added to the team's total.

Additional runs can be gained by the batting team as extras (called "sundries" in Australia) due to errors made by the fielding side. This is achieved in four ways: no-ball, a penalty of one extra conceded by the bowler if he breaks the rules; wide, a penalty of one extra conceded by the bowler if he bowls so that the ball is out of the batter's reach bye, an extra awarded if the batter misses the ball and it goes past the wicket-keeper and gives the batters time to run in the conventional way leg bye, as for a bye except that the ball has hit the batter's body, though not his bat. If the bowler has conceded a no-ball or a wide, his team incurs an additional penalty because that ball (i.e., delivery) has to be bowled again and hence the batting side has the opportunity to score more runs from this extra ball.

- Specialist roles

Captain (cricket) and Wicket-keeper
The captain is often the most experienced player in the team, certainly the most tactically astute, and can possess any of the main skillsets as a batter, a bowler or a wicket-keeper. Within the Laws, the captain has certain responsibilities in terms of nominating his players to the umpires before the match and ensuring that his players conduct themselves "within the spirit and traditions of the game as well as within the Laws".

The wicket-keeper (sometimes called simply the "keeper") is a specialist fielder subject to various rules within the Laws about his equipment and demeanour. He is the only member of the fielding side who can effect a stumping and is the only one permitted to wear gloves and external leg guards. Depending on their primary skills, the other ten players in the team tend to be classified as specialist batters or specialist bowlers. Generally, a team will include five or six specialist batters and four or five specialist bowlers, plus the wicket-keeper.

- Umpires and scorers

Umpire (cricket), Scoring (cricket), and Cricket statistics
An umpire signals a decision to the scorers
The game on the field is regulated by the two umpires, one of whom stands behind the wicket at the bowler's end, the other in a position called "square leg" which is about 15–20 metres away from the batter on strike and in line with the popping crease on which he is taking guard. The umpires have several responsibilities including adjudication on whether a ball has been correctly bowled (i.e., not a no-ball or a wide); when a run is scored; whether a batter is out (the fielding side must first appeal to the umpire, usually with the phrase "How's that?" or "Owzat?"); when intervals start and end; and the suitability of the pitch, field and weather for playing the game. The umpires are authorised to interrupt or even abandon a match due to circumstances likely to endanger the players, such as a damp pitch or deterioration of the light.

Off the field in televised matches, there is usually a third umpire who can make decisions on certain incidents with the aid of video evidence. The third umpire is mandatory under the playing conditions for Test and Limited Overs International matches played between two ICC full member countries. These matches also have a match referee whose job is to ensure that play is within the Laws and the spirit of the game.

The match details, including runs and dismissals, are recorded by two official scorers, one representing each team. The scorers are directed by the hand signals of an umpire . For example, the umpire raises a forefinger to signal that the batter is out (has been dismissed); he raises both arms above his head if the batter has hit the ball for six runs. The scorers are required by the Laws to record all runs scored, wickets taken and overs bowled; in practice, they also note significant amounts of additional data relating to the game.

A match's statistics are summarised on a scorecard. Prior to the popularisation of scorecards, most scoring was done by men sitting on vantage points cuttings notches on tally sticks and runs were originally called notches.According to Rowland Bowen, the earliest known scorecard templates were introduced in 1776 by T. Pratt of Sevenoaks and soon came into general use.It is believed that scorecards were printed and sold at Lord's for the first time in 1846.

- thank you for buy & read this book

have a great day of your
from : Mr Vivek Kumar Pandey